Hamilton, John   623.7
                                   H

Humvees

MILITARY VEHICLES
HUMVEES
BY JOHN HAMILTON

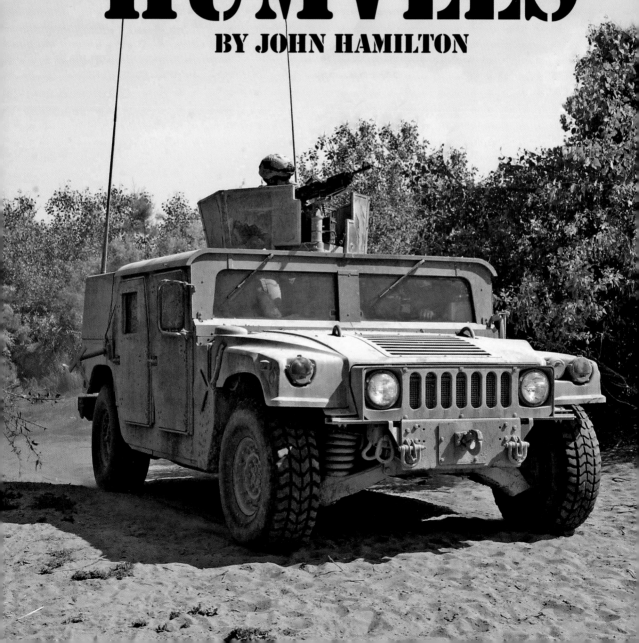

VISIT US AT
WWW.ABDOPUBLISHING.COM

Published by ABDO Publishing Company, 8000 West 78th Street, Suite 310, Edina, MN 55439. Copyright ©2012 by Abdo Consulting Group, Inc. International copyrights reserved in all countries. No part of this book may be reproduced in any form without written permission from the publisher. A&D Xtreme™ is a trademark and logo of ABDO Publishing Company.

Printed in the United States of America, North Mankato, Minnesota.
062011
092011

PRINTED ON RECYCLED PAPER

Editor: Sue Hamilton
Graphic Design: Sue Hamilton
Cover Design: John Hamilton
Cover Photo: Getty Images
Interior Photos: AM General-pgs 12-13 & 20-21; AP-pg 8; BAE Systems-pg 29; Corbis-pg 9; Defense Video & Imagery Distribution System-pgs 1-5, 26 (insert), 28, 30-31; Department of Defense-pgs 6-7, 10, 11, 16-19, 22 (insert), 22-25; United States Marines-pgs 26-27; United States Navy-pgs 14-15, & 32.

Library of Congress Cataloging-in-Publication Data

Hamilton, John, 1959-
  Humvees / John Hamilton.
      p. cm.
  Includes index.
  Audience: Ages 8-15.
  ISBN 978-1-61783-076-1
  1. Hummer trucks--Juvenile literature. 2. Military trucks--United States--Juvenile literature.
  1. Hummer trucks. 2. Trucks.] I. Title.
  UG618.H358 2011
  623.7'4722--dc23
                              2011020093

TABLE OF CONTENTS

★ HUMVEES ★

The High Mobility Multipurpose Wheeled Vehicle (HMMWV) is the workhorse of today's United States Army and other military services. Many people call it by its nickname: the Humvee. Compared to most military vehicles, the Humvee is light and highly mobile.

More than 60 nations besides the United States use Humvees in their military services.

HMMWV FAST FACTS

Humvees are used by all branches of the United States military. The Army, Navy, Air Force, Marines, and Coast Guard use these multipurpose vehicles as reliable transportation in all types of weather and over all types of terrain.

Humvee M998
Cargo/Troop Carrier
Specifications

Length:	15 feet (4.6 m)
Width:	7 feet, 2 inches (2.2 m)
Height:	6 feet (1.8 m)
Weight:	5,200 pounds (2,359 kg)
Engine:	V8, 6.2 liter displacement
Transmission:	3-speed automatic
Top Speed:	65 miles per hour (105 kph)
Cruising Range:	350 miles (563 km)
Manufacturer:	AM General

HISTORY

During World War II, the U.S. Army relied on the jeep, a small, tough vehicle that could carry troops through almost any terrain. More than 640,000 were built during the war.

Where did the name "jeep" come from? One story says that the Army called the original jeep a "General Purpose" vehicle. Soldiers sounded out the "GP" and simply called the vehicle a "jeep."

XTREME FACT

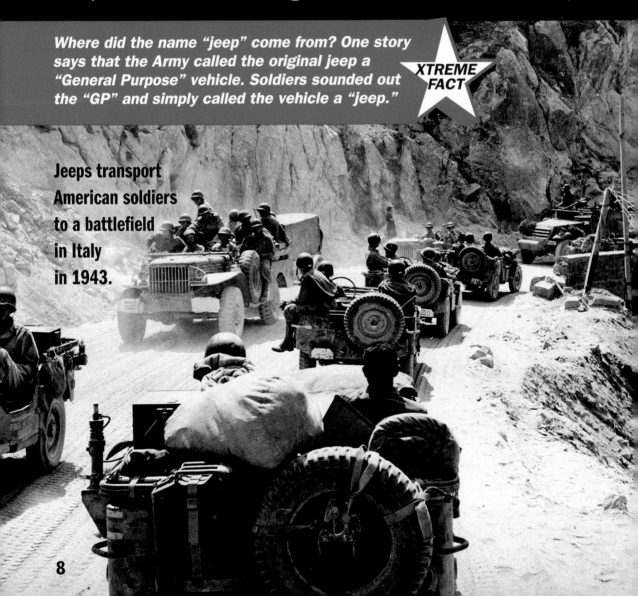

Jeeps transport American soldiers to a battlefield in Italy in 1943.

As modern warfare evolved, the Army needed a vehicle that was even more rugged and could carry heavier loads. The Humvee is a replacement for the Army's M151 series jeep and other light utility vehicles. The Humvee entered service in 1985. To date, more than 190,000 Humvees have been built.

An early model High Mobility Multipurpose Wheeled Vehicle (HMMWV).

VERSIONS

The Humvee currently has 15 configurations. Most versions use a common chassis, transmission, engine, and many other parts. The Humvee can be used as a troop and cargo carrier, weapons platform, communications dish carrier, ambulance and scout vehicle. It can even be modified with tracks to run in the snow.

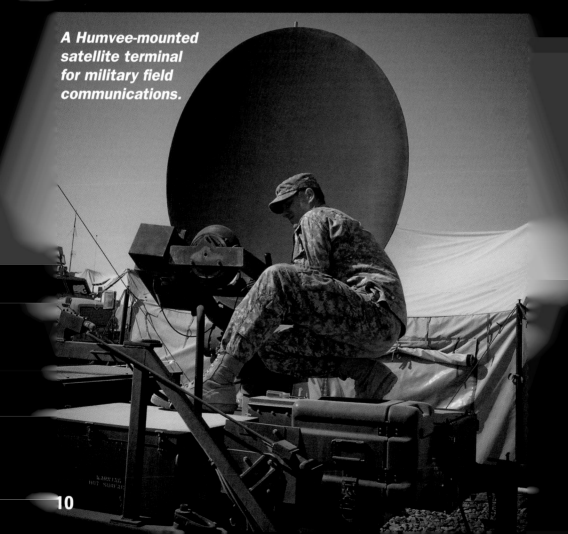

A Humvee-mounted satellite terminal for military field communications.

A Humvee ambulance.

A Humvee with snow tracks.

SUSPENSION AND TIRES

The Humvee has four-wheel independent suspension, with full-time four-wheel drive. The rugged suspension helps it drive through almost any terrain, including sand, snow, and mud. It can climb slopes at a very steep angle.

The Humvee's big tires are set wide apart, making it very stable. The vehicle's low profile helps it hug the road. Stability is critical when driving over rough terrain, or when speeding around corners.

XTREME FACT

The Humvee uses "runflat" radial tires, which can be used for up to 30 miles (48 km) when damaged or deflated.

CHASSIS AND BODY

The Humvee's strong chassis is a framework made of high-grade alloy steel. Aluminum body panels are held together and attached to the chassis by high-tech adhesives and rivets. The body is designed to be flexible. This helps it stay intact during the stress of off-road travel.

Rivets help hold a Hummer's body panels and chassis together.

GROUND CLEARANCE

United States soldiers drive a Humvee over extremely rough and steep terrain.

The Humvee's chassis sits very high. The vehicle's ground clearance (the distance between the ground and the chassis) is 16 inches (41 cm). The Humvee can roll right over many obstacles, including small boulders.

ENGINE AND TRANSMISSION

The M998-series Humvee is powered by a 6.2-liter eight-cylinder diesel engine. It uses a three-speed automatic transmission. The engine weighs about 650 pounds (295 kg). It is very reliable and tough. It can be serviced and repaired quickly. This is especially important when operating in remote battlefields of the world, like Iraq or Afghanistan.

A U.S. Air Force maintenance mechanic stationed in Iraq checks a Humvee's engine.

CARGO CAPACITY

Humvees are designed to carry heavy loads. The model M1113 Expanded Capacity Vehicle (ECV) has a payload of 5,100 pounds (2,313 kg). That is almost as much weight as the vehicle itself, which tips the scales at 6,400 pounds (2,903 kg). The ECV uses a more-powerful turbocharged 6.5-liter V8 diesel engine that generates 190 horsepower.

AIR TRANSPORT

The modern U.S. Army stresses rapid response to today's global threats. That means transporting soldiers and equipment to the battlefield as quickly as possible. Humvees can be sling-loaded by helicopters and ferried to their destination. Up to 15 Humvees can be loaded into a C-5A Galaxy transport plane.

Humvees are unloaded from a Galaxy transport plane in Somalia.

Humvees can also be directly dropped by parachute into combat zones that are too dangerous for planes or helicopters to land.

A Chinook helicopter transports a Humvee to a U.S. Army base in Afghanistan in 2010.

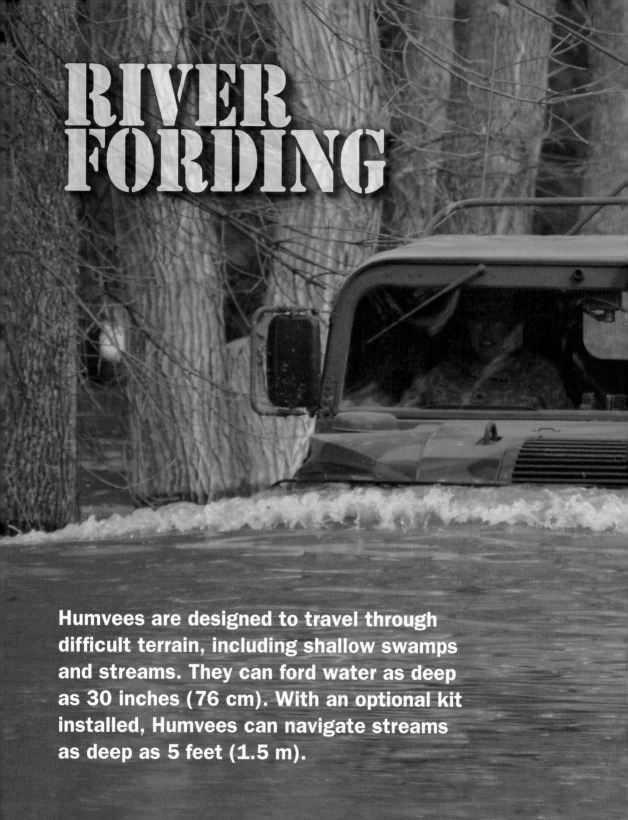

RIVER FORDING

Humvees are designed to travel through difficult terrain, including shallow swamps and streams. They can ford water as deep as 30 inches (76 cm). With an optional kit installed, Humvees can navigate streams as deep as 5 feet (1.5 m).

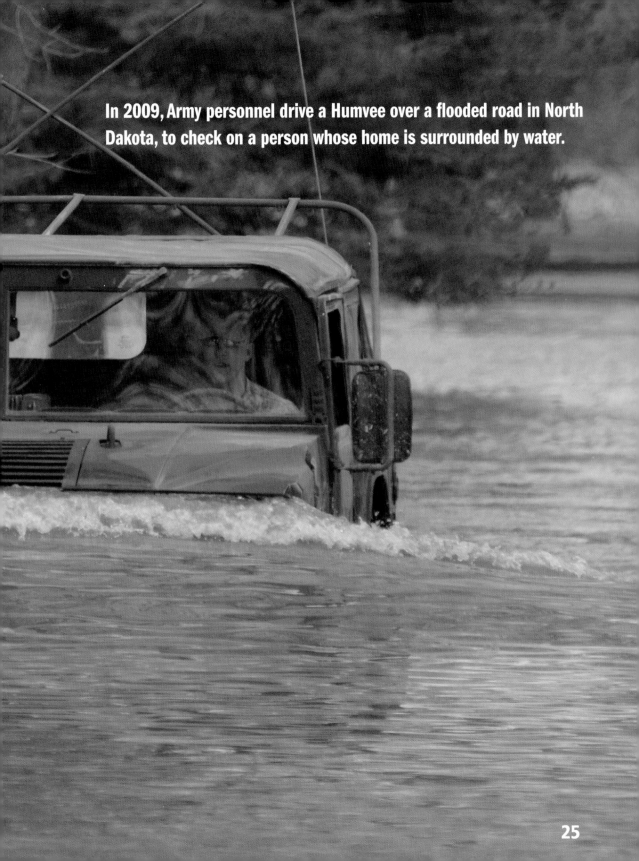

In 2009, Army personnel drive a Humvee over a flooded road in North Dakota, to check on a person whose home is surrounded by water.

WEAPONS

A .50-caliber machine gun mounted on a Humvee.

Humvees were designed mainly to haul soldiers and equipment. But they can be modified to act as a weapons platform, with soldiers operating equipment such as an M2 heavy machine gun or Mk 19 grenade launcher.

XTREME FACT

Humvees can also be modified to carry and fire TOW missiles, which are used against tanks and other armored vehicles.

A Tube-Launched, Optically Tracked Wire-Guided (TOW) missile is fired from a HMMWV turret.

THE FUTURE

Humvees are especially vulnerable to mines, heavy weapons, and improvised explosive devices (IEDs). To counter that risk, some Humvees receive an up-armor upgrade. Up-armored Humvees include extra protection against these threats, but the additional weight makes them less maneuverable.

Up-armored Humvees give soldiers additional protection against explosives.

The U.S. military's future Joint Light Tactical Vehicle (JLTV) is designed from the ground up to be an armored scout vehicle that can better survive the dangers of today's battlefield, including mines and other explosives. It will likely someday replace most Humvees. Until that time, the Humvee will remain a reliable military workhorse for years to come.

GLOSSARY

ALLOY STEEL

A type of steel to which additional elements have been added to make it stronger, harder, and more wear-resistant. This type of steel is used in Humvees to help it handle the stress of off-road travel.

ARMOR

A strong, protective covering made to protect military vehicles.

CHASSIS

The internal framework of a vehicle that supports the body, engine, transmission, and suspension.

COMBAT ZONE

An area where military fighting takes place.

DIESEL FUEL

A thick petroleum product that is used in diesel engines, such as those found in heavy tanks, trucks, and Humvees.

GRENADE

A bomb with a delayed explosion thrown by hand or shot from a rifle or launcher.

Suspension

The system of springs and shock absorbers that connect a vehicle to its wheels. The Humvee has four-wheel independent suspension, which means each of its four wheels can turn independent of one another. This helps it move through slippery terrain like snow, sand, or mud.

Transmission

The parts of a vehicle that sends or "transmits" power from the engine to the wheels to make it move.

Turbocharge

To add additional power to an engine to make it move faster than it normally would be able to move.

Turret

The top part of a military vehicle, which houses the main weapons. The turret rotates, allowing a gunner to aim and fire in any direction.

World War II

A war that was fought from 1939 to 1945, involving countries around the world. The United States entered the war after Japan's bombing of the American naval base at Pearl Harbor, in Oahu, Hawaii, on December 7, 1941.

INDEX